Sugar Rehab

Staying Fit and Young by Overcoming Your Secret Addiction to Sugar

DR. GERALD EDELMAN, MD, PHD

Carpenter's Son Publishing

Sugar Rehab: Staying Fit and Young by Overcoming Your Secret Addiction to Sugar

Published by Carpenter's Son Publishing, Franklin, Tennessee

Cover and Interior Design by Suzanne Lawing

Edited by Tammy Kling

Printed in the United States of America

978-1-940262-20-8

Contents

Foreword

Living a Healthy Life

Tony Jeary

When I first read this book, I couldn't put it down. I read through it in a couple of hours without stopping, because it fascinated me. When a cancer doctor writes a book, you ought to listen. Right?

Dr. Edelman and I met at another doctor's house over dinner, and immediately connected. That day turned into a friendship and it evolved even more when I discovered that that he wasn't just an oncologist, but that he had a passion for helping people live longer, happier, and healthier lives.

There are two distinctions in this book that I would like to point out right away.

One is the focus on reducing sugar, and two is the focus on reducing cardiovascular activity and increasing exercise in the form of lifting weights, to impact muscle and strength.

So many people think sugar is about the calories. But Dr. Edelman reveals the truth.

The problem with sugar really is about the insulin spike you get, and the impact on your glycemic index.

If you understand GI and the impact it has on your health, it will equip you to make better decisions in everyday life.

I've published 40 books and advised over a thousand companies including personally coaching the presidents of Walmart, Shell, Ford, Firestone, Samsung and even people on the richest list on Forbes. And, I constantly study the best of the best - and what I've found is that even though high achievers are different we are all chemically the same. Dr Edelman's book can help you understand your body chemistry in order to make the right decisions.

Introduction

How young do you feel? When it comes right down to it, no matter how old we are, we all want to feel (and look) younger, biologically, physically, and emotionally. Now that I'm in my 50's, much of my focus has turned to staying young. I'm not talking about 5 or 10 years younger. I'm talking about 20 years younger!

Feel free to think I'm crazy for now. You might also want to admit, where there's a will, there's a way. It all starts with a state of mind. As adults, we are pressured to mentally give up less than halfway through our lives. We are told to give up on our looks because those fade. We are told to give up playing music because we'll never be famous. We won't write a book or visit the moon or end human suffering. It is as if these endeavors are only worthwhile if we fully succeed, as if exploration is pointless. The only two priorities we are *allowed* to have are a family and a career.

Don't get me wrong, these are great priorities! A happy family and a successful career are important pieces to the puzzle of life. The problem is that most of us feel guilty when we actually make time for ourselves. Any time spent on a "hobby" is time we could have spent with our family or making money. We need to realize that we are programmed to think this way. Taking time for ourselves doesn't actually hurt our kids, our spouses, or our wallets. It does allow us to decompress, to focus our passion on something other than work and family. What we do defines us. Keeping sight of personal dreams nurtures the instincts of our children, and it makes loving our families and careers easier.

Rather than promote self-fulfillment, society pressures us into thinking "old." We spend our days rushing around, focused on others and steadily losing sleep. The lack of sleep and personal time catches up, and our youth disappears.

This book will help you rediscover your youth, both mentally and physically. Many men and women who are enthusiastic about life appear to be younger than their actual age. This comes as no surprise. If you ask them, these same men and women openly say they feel young. It is as if their thoughts and feelings influence their physical appearance.

Is it possible that if you think old, you will look old? I certainly don't want to grow old anytime soon. If there's any chance of this being true, I want to think like a kid. I want to cultivate that youthful curiosity, passion, and joy in my life. If anything, I'll certainly be happy.

To help achieve this, I resist cultural stress and center myself with positive thoughts. I also try to be aware of harmful or negative thoughts. The more aware you are, the more you will be able to control your thoughts. You will be more likely to have healthy relationships. You must realize: for every negative thought, there is an opposite, positive thought. Creating a reality in your mind that views the glass as half full will facilitate your energy levels. That same energy draws people to you because it's something they want to be a part of. Positive energy makes you attractive to others.

You must be aware of when it's okay to behave like a goofy kid and when it is necessary to be responsible. You need both discipline and non-conformity. Practice discipline in your lifestyle choices, and learn to resist societal definitions of how you should think. This will help you attain a longer, high-quality life that encourages youthful vitality.

Being a non-conformist requires courage and intelligence. Look around you. How many adults are in shape and mentally happy? Very few people retain youthful qualities into adulthood. Many people neglect sensible habits, such as a good night's sleep, regular exercise, and healthy eating. A lack of time and energy is the most common excuse.

Missing out on sleep, physical activity, and well-balanced meals only makes us *more* tired. The more exhausted we become, the less we care about how we look and feel. Stress consumes our day-to-day emotions and we physically appear unwell. We try to cope, but we end up hiding from our problems. We lose interest in our own lives, blankly staring from the sidelines as if we are already dead. It is as if living has escaped us.

But, we are not dead.

It's time to throw away the excuses. We've identified the will, now here's the way.

Within these pages, I hope to offer a way to increase your youthful feeling and vitality.

A lot of the information in this book might seem radical, but it's based on my years of work practicing as a physician. I've seen a lot of patients who were unhealthy because of their own habits and lifestyle. It's difficult as a doctor who wants to heal people, to work with patients who work against themselves.

If a patient arrives with obesity, diabetes, or some other disease and won't exercise or eat well, the entire healing regimen won't work.

This book is designed to help increase your youthful vitality and bring healthy habits back into your life. At times, I'll be busting myths you've heard along the way. Some, even from the medical profession.

One is that red wine is good for your health and that it's okay to drink.

It may be true that red wine has some positive health benefits including increased longevity. This is thought to be because red wine contains the chemical reservatrol which is thought to protect cells from injury and increase cellular energy. Because red wine increases your blood sugar and is higher on the glycemic index, I would suggest if you want to get reservatrol, you should get it as a supplement in pill form.

You may have heard that it's okay to drink. And, I'm not here to dispute that if that's in your lifestyle. But I want to teach you how to drink well.

In this book there's a chapter on alcohol consumption that will teach you what to drink to reduce sugar intake. (It's not wine!)

I have a PhD in molecular and cellular biology and my life's work is dedicated to understanding the body.

I do cancer research and have authored fifteen-plus articles on new drugs for cancer prevention. When I see patients, I must listen, and then coach them toward the appropriate solution.

My philosophy in doctoring is to get rid of myself and become a good listener.

Because it's a cancer practice, 30% of my patients are dealing with death. It can't be explained and it can't be postponed anymore, and the patient and the family members must face it head on. This isn't a fun process; it's horrible, in fact, and I wish to do everything I can to help individuals live longer, healthier lives. Sadly, 50% of my patients are obese. They come to me with obesity-related illnesses and then the solution involves treating the illnesses, created by excess weight and poor daily nutritional and eating habits.

In any doctor's practice 80% of the problems are the result of obesity. Throughout all of my years practicing medicine I learned that there's cumulative clinical data that higher sugar levels correlate to higher levels of cancer. Insulin does stimulate cancer. So what can we do? One thing, is to reduce sugar intake. The link between sugar and cancer and cancer is direct. It's a toxin. And, we don't burn it off. Sugar remains in our cells. It is not metabolizing quickly in your body. So do all you can to reduce your sugar, and balance your blood system. Exercise regularly, but don't overdo it. And most of all, enjoy your life!

This book works because it's simple. It works for how you look, how you feel, and how you live.

CHAPTER 1

What is the Glycemic Index? (And how does it affect your life?)

Understanding your body and how it works is important. There is a science to be learned. It is important to understand the process of insulin secretion. Insulin is a hormone created by the pancreas that helps regulate some metabolic functions. It is released in cycles throughout the day, but amounts of insulin spike shortly after eating. Foods that cause high insulin levels contain large amounts of sugar. High-sugar foods are classified as high-glycemic items on the Glycemic Index.

You need to stay away from high-sugar foods. Why? They make you fat! The excess sugar simply isn't good for you. It can contribute to a lot more than weight gain, including coronary artery disease, stroke, high cholesterol, and energy or mood swings.

Taking control of your health doesn't require weighing food or counting calories. It doesn't require starving yourself. You just need to understand the reasons why some foods are okay to eat and some should be avoided. The way low-sugar and high-sugar foods interact is also important.

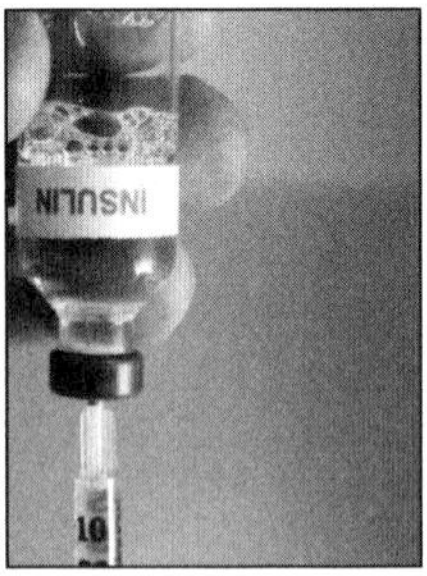

The Glycemic Index refers to the relationship between a food item and the amount of insulin that your pancreas releases if you eat that item. Insulin controls your body's carbohydrate and fat metabolism. When insulin is released, your body absorbs sugar from your blood. The specific type of sugar that it takes in is called glucose. This sugar is stored within your liver, muscle, and fat cells.

Insulin also stops your body from burning stored fat as a fuel source. This means that tissues in your body take in sugar. They metabolize, or "burn" the sugar, for fuel. Any leftover sugar is stored as a secondary energy source. Your fat, that was stored as your body's main energy supply, is not burned.

Are you starting to see the problem here? Stored fat is supposed to be the body's go-to source of energy between meals. It is metabolized at a slow, steady pace. This way, the body does not experience a sudden surge or drop in energy levels. Insulin prevents this process from happening. Large amounts of sugar cause large amounts of insulin. The large amounts of insulin cause the very high and low energy extremes.

During a sugar high, your body is functioning much faster than it needs to be. It is like your body is rapidly aging because it is living in the fast lane. Then, out of nowhere, your energy plummets. You feel exhausted, and you need something to help wake you up. So you reach for more food. With so much insulin already in your bloodstream, your brain automatically tells you to reach for something with sugar.

What I am telling you is earth-shattering for many people. Fat is not bad. Fat is not the enemy. Insulin is not actually the enemy either, since it is necessary to regulate certain bodily functions. If insulin allowed the excess sugar to remain in your bloodstream, it would become toxic.

Sugar is the enemy.

If you are still skeptical, consider the combination of a high-fat food with a high-sugar food. When eaten alone, the high-fat food will allow for slow digestion and absorption. This gives your body a steady amount of energy. When a high-sugar food is eaten alone, your body will quickly absorb the fuel. This causes extreme high and low energy levels.

When eaten together, a high-fat and high-sugar meal will be digested more quickly. A large amount of fat will be stored, instead of supplying balanced energy. This is where cholesterol becomes a real health issue. On top of that, the excess sugar will cause intense energy swings. To stay awake, you will reach for more high-sugar foods.

This whole process means you are likely to gain weight. The weight will be gained through the storage of fats and sugars, instead of building lean muscle. It will also increase your levels of cholesterol, causing increasing health risks. Once you understand this, it will be easier to prefer only low-glycemic and low-sugar foods.

Master Food List

Here is your master-list of Okay and Not Okay foods for stocking your kitchen. Foods that include a Limited label should be consumed in moderation. I avoid eating Limited-labeled food items, fruit, or anything sweet at night.

Above all else, use common sense. Sugar from any source is your enemy.

Okay List	Not Okay List
FRUITS	
Apples	All Candied Fruits
Apricots (Limited)	All Dried Fruits
Avocados	All Fruit Juices
Bananas (Limited, preferably under-ripe)	Canned Fruit

Blackberries	Dates
Blueberries	Figs
Cantaloupe	Frozen Fruit (with added sugar)
Cherries (Limited)	Fruit Cups
Frozen Fruit (no sugar added)	Fruit Snacks
Grapefruit	Grapes
Green Plantains (Limited)	Pineapple
Honeydew Melon	Prunes
Kiwi	Raisins
Kumquat (Limited)	Watermelon
Lemon (just a splash)	
Lime (just a splash)	
Mango (Limited)	
Nectarines (Limited)	
Olives	
Oranges (Limited)	
Peaches (Limited)	
Pear	
Persimmons (Limited)	
Plums (Limited)	
Raspberries	
Strawberries	
Tangerines (Limited)	
Tomatoes	

VEGETABLES	
Alfalfa Sprouts	All Corn
Artichoke	All Potatoes
Arugula	Canned Vegetables (in sauce with sugar)
Asparagus	Frozen Vegetables (in sauce with sugar)
Bean Sprouts	Yams
Broccoli	

Beets	
Bok Choy	
Brussels Sprouts	
Cabbage	
Carrots	
Cauliflower	
Celery	
Cucumber	
Eggplant	
Endive	
Frozen Vegetables (no sauce or sugar-free sauce)	
Garlic	
Ginger	
Green Beans	
Herbs	
Leeks	
Lettuce	
Mushrooms	
Onions	
Parsley	
Peppers	
Pickles	
Radishes	
Scallions	
Shallots	
Snap Peas	
Spinach	
Squash	
Turnips	
Vegetable Medley	
Vegetable Party Platter	
Zucchini	

BEANS, NUTS, LEGUMES	
Almonds	Baked Beans (in sweet sauce)
Almond Butter	Broad Beans
Black Beans	
Black-Eyed Peas	
Brazil Nuts	
Butter Beans	
Cannellini Beans	
Cashews	
Chestnuts	
Chickpeas	
Garbanzo Beans	
Haricot Beans	
Hazelnuts	
Hummus	
Kidney Beans (white, dark, and red)	
Lentils (brown, green, and red)	
Lima Beans	
Macadamia Nuts	
Marrow Fat Peas	
Mixed Nuts	
Mung Beans	
Navy Beans	
Peanuts	
Peanut Butter	
Peas	
Pigeon Peas	
Pinto Beans	
Pistachios	
Soya Beans	
Split Peas	
Tofu	
Walnuts	

Lobster	
Mackerel	
Oysters	
Pheasant	
Pork (preferably lean)	
Red Snapper	
Salmon	
Sausage (preferably lean)	
Shark Steak	
Shrimp	
Slim-Fast Low-Carb Shake (Limited)	
Tuna	
Turkey	
Veal	
Venison	
Whiting	

SNACKS, SWEETS, SAUCES, CONDIMENTS	
Any Cream Sauce	A1 Steak Sauce
Any Low-Sugar/No-Sugar Sauce	All Bakery Sweets
Guacamole (no sugar added)	All Candy
Hard-Boiled Eggs	All Carmel
Horseradish	All Chocolate
Hot Sauce (no sugar added, check label for sugar contents)	All Pre-Made Dough for Cooking
Hummus	All Sauces with Added Sugar
Jell-O (only sugar-free)	All Types of Sugar
Relish (non-sweet, no sugar added)	Bagel Bites
Mustard	Barbeque Sauce
Mayonnaise	Cake
Real Cheese Dips	Candied Fruit
Rice Cakes (Limited)	Candied Nuts
Roasted and Lightly Salted Nuts	Chips

Salsa (homemade, no sugar added)	Chip Dip
Splenda	Cocktail Sauce
Soy Sauce (preferably low-sodium)	Coffee-Mate Creamer
Stevia	Cookie Dough
Sweet 'n Low	Cookies
Tartar Sauce (no sugar added)	Crackers (even whole grain)
Vegetable Dip (no sugar added)	Dressing (with sugar added)
Wasabi	Dried Fruits
Whole-Fat Dressings (no sugar added)	Fake Cheese Spreads
Whole Whipped Cream (Limited)	Flavored Creamers
Whole Sour Cream	Frozen Breakfast Snacks
	Frozen Party Snacks
	Fruit Spreads
	Graham Crackers
	Honey
	Hot Pockets
	Hot Sauce (with sugar added)
	Jell-O (with sugar added)
	Jelly (including low-sugar and no-sugar added)
	Ketchup
	Lean Pockets
	Mashed Potatoes
	Nutella
	Pastries
	Pies (crusts and fillings)
	Pizza (pre-made and crusts)
	Popsicles (even sugar-free)
	Pop-Tarts
	Pudding
	Raisins
	Syrup
	Toaster Strudel

	Vinaigrette Dressing (with sugar added)
	Wine Sauces
	Yogurt

BEVERAGES, ALCOHOLIC AND NON-ALCOHOLIC	
Bourbon	All Fruit Juices
Coffee	All Regular Beers
Crown Royal	Apple Juice
Crystal Light	Chocolate Milk
Diet Soda	Coconut Water
Fresca	Cosmo Mixes
Gin	Cranberry Juice
Ultra-Light Beer (Limited)	Daiquiris
V8 Tomato Juice (Limited, no sugar added)	Drinks Containing Pre-Made Mixes (both alcoholic and non-alcoholic)
Vodka	Frozen Alcoholic Beverages
Water	Frozen Juices
Whiskey	Grape Juice
Wine (Very Limited)	Hurricane Mixes
	Margarita Mixes
	Mojito Mixes
	Old-Fashioned Mixes
	Orange Juice
	Pina Coladas
	Pineapple Juice
	Regular Soda
	Regular Tonic
	Sake
	Shakes
	Simple Syrup
	Smoothies
	V8 Splash

CHAPTER 2

Are Diets Good for You?

There are some pretty smart dieting plans out there. The Paleo or Paleolithic Diet claims that you should eat like our human ancestors because your body is programmed the same way. This is true, but today's society leads a much more sedentary lifestyle than it once did. You can't eat the same foods when you aren't doing the same work.

The Warrior Diet offers a similar basis on human heritage. It indicates that you need to eat very little throughout the day, but you must eat one large meal at night. Perhaps if you were moving all day, this diet may work long-term. However, when you are stuck at a desk most of the day, you need to keep your metabolism up. If you do not eat until right before bed, your metabolism will run very low until the time you are ready to fall asleep. This is the opposite of what anyone working in an office truly needs.

The South Beach Diet gets a lot of things right. It preaches the difference between good carbs vs. bad carbs and good fats vs. bad fats. This is

all great information to know, but the way the diet is broken down can get confusing. It's almost as if the book provides too much information, frustrating the reader with details. The important points become lost. In my opinion, the South Beach Diet also does not place enough emphasis on downsizing sugar intake.

Finally, the Atkins Diet is very popular for its intense emphasis on carbohydrate restriction. This is a smart diet, but it is not necessary to restrict all carbohydrate consumption to such an extreme. Fiber and whole grains are good for you. It's just a serious effort to find sources of real grain in today's supermarkets.

Some doctors may say that diets aren't good because getting fit is about a "lifestyle." True, your lifestyle and habits are important. But when I see an obese patient facing illness—the first prescribed regimen is a plan to lose excess weight.

Defining a Diet and Why it Can Fail

You may be thinking to yourself, "Hmm, it seems as if this book is taking pieces of mainstream diets and throwing them all together to make one super-diet!"

You may be partially right, and partially wrong.

I do not like the word "diet." Technically, diet simply indicates the foods that you eat on a regular basis. Your diet could be made up entirely of cookies, and it would still be called a diet. A diet is just what you eat. The problem is, when people say they are on a "diet," they mean that they are temporarily eating healthier to lose weight.

A healthy diet should never be something temporary. It should be a life-long effort to maintain your strength, youth, and physique. It can also set a good example for your children.

This is why you will not see the word "diet" throughout this book. I am teaching you how your body digests food, and I am teaching you how to work with that. You are learning how to maximize your metabolism, so you can minimize your waist. I am teaching you to be healthier, to feel younger and more energized. What I am teaching you is not meant to be finite, it is meant to be with you for the rest of your life. It is a new way of looking at food, and it is a new way of living. It is a new way of keeping your inner youth, to help you put your best foot forward.

Other "diets" have failed because you saw them as diets. You viewed them as temporary attempts at being healthier. You probably started these other diets in preparation for a big event. Once that event passed, you eventually fell off the wagon and began searching for a new diet to try.

You have to stop dieting.

Yes, this is your new diet, and this is the last time I will call it a diet. It is your new lifestyle. It is going to help rebuild the parts of your life that you are unhappy with.

Diet Quiz

1. Which type of cuisine should you avoid at all costs?

a. Italian
b. Mexican
c. Seafood
d. Barbeque
e. None of the above

2. What is the basis of the Paleo or Paleolithic Diet?

a. This diet suggests that you should hunt and gather your own food.
b. This diet lets you eat plenty of bread.
c. This diet suggests that your body is adapted to the foods eaten by the early human species.
d. This diet doesn't let you eat any type of seafood.
e. None of the above.

3. If you began the Warrior Diet, you would:

a. Eat whatever you wanted all day long.
b. Be prepared to go to war.
c. Eat only meat, cheese, nuts, and other sources of protein.
d. Eat very little throughout the day and eat one large meal at night.
e. None of the above.

4. The South Beach Diet is famous for:

a. Its hometown location of South Beach, Florida.
b. Its good-carbs vs. bad-carbs and good-fats vs. bad-fats take on dieting.
c. The way it motivates women to fit into tiny bikinis.
d. Allowing as much alcohol consumption as desired, at all times.
e. None of the above.

5. In his book *Dr. Atkins' New Diet Revolution,* Dr. Atkins asserts that:

a. Seafood is unhealthy for you.
b. You still need enough fruits and vegetables to balance the protein in your diet.
c. Eating any type of fat will make you gain weight.
d. A low-carb diet increases your resting metabolism because it takes more calories for your body to burn fat.
e. None of the above.

TRUE OR FALSE

6. Low fat chocolate milk is healthier than cream.

7. Rice is okay to eat, just make sure it is whole-grain.

8. Your body processes more cholesterol when it is consumed with high-sugar foods.

9. A fruit smoothie is often loaded with added sugar.

10. Fried foods are okay to eat because they do not have tons of sugar.

11. If you drink alcohol, just make sure to drink clear liquors.

12. It is okay if you are busy and have to skip a meal.

13. You can eat any steak, any way you like it.

14. Candied carrots are okay to eat because they're at least a vegetable.

15. If you eat Mexican food, chips and salsa are good to load up on because tomatoes are healthy.

16. Which is better to drink:

a. One ultra-light beer
b. One small order of house sake

17. Which is better to eat:

a. Pineapple

b. Carrots

18. Which is better to eat:

a. Creamed spinach

b. Candied nuts

19. Which is better to eat:

a. Lots of fruits and vegetables with some long-grain rice

b. Lamb with roasted peppers and a heavy cream sauce

20. Which is better to eat:

a. Cherries

b. Grapes

21. Which is worse to eat:

a. Cantaloupe

b. Corn

22. Which is worse to eat:

a. Bacon

b. Potato

23. Which is worse to eat:

a. Low-carb ice cream

b. Aged cheese

24. Which is worse to eat:

a. Pizza

b. Veal marsala

25. Which is worse to eat:

a. Hibachi-cooked foods without rice

b. Sushi and small seaweed salad

CHAPTER 3

Combining Foods

Stay away from high-fat, high-sugar recipes. Eggs, for example, are a great food when eaten alone or with other low-sugar foods. They offer lots of B-vitamins, protein, choline, and vitamin D. Make sure you eat the yokes because that is where all these nutrients are!

On the other hand, if you eat eggs with high-sugar foods, the eggs become unhealthy. Common high-sugar foods include hash browns, potatoes, and certain breads. Your body will always digest the sugars in these foods first. The sugar is easier and quicker to metabolize. By the time your body gets around to the protein-rich eggs, it thinks that you are already full. Not only do the egg's protein and fats get stored, but so does the cholesterol.

Unfortunately, that sugar-buzz wears off quickly. Plenty of insulin is already in your bloodstream and your body assumes you must be hungry again. It asks you to reach for more high-sugar choices instead of burning the eggs that it stored as fat earlier.

More Examples of Harmful Meal Choices

If you want to eat heartily without the weight gain, you have to understand this process completely. You can mix foods on the Okay List to come up with your own meals and snacks. You must avoid, almost obsessively, the foods on the Not Okay List.

The high-sugar foods on the Not Okay List cause a large insulin spike in the bloodstream. Pastas, for example, release a serious amount of insulin. Pasta is frequently eaten with high-fat meats and cheeses as well. If these meats or cheeses were consumed alone, the fat would be digested for fuel. In the case of spaghetti and meatballs, the pasta digests quicker, so it is used for fuel. The meats and cheeses are then stored as fat.

Pizza is another example of a horrible high-fat, high-sugar food. It is harmful because the crust is digested first, causing a lofty insulin spike. The cheese and meat toppings are stored as fat. Those same high-fat toppings, if consumed alone or with other foods on the Okay List, are not fattening.

You end up feeling lethargic after your body has soaked up all the excess sugar. You are bloated because you stored a bunch of fat. Your cholesterol levels are elevated. This all contributes to feeling "old" and unwell. If you actually wanted to feel that way, you wouldn't be reading this book.

Restaurant Dining

Dining out can be a challenge, but using the following guidelines will help you make the right decisions. I recommend that you don't indulge in wine or beer for the first six months of your new lifestyle. If you do drink, order a cocktail from the Okay List of alcoholic beverages. Make sure to emphasize that you do not want any sugar or syrup in your drink. Calories are not of concern here.

My drink of choice when dining out is vodka with soda water (Diet Sprite at home), a splash of lime, some mint, and Splenda. This is a low-sugar beverage called a Vodka Mohita. It is best not to order it by name because syrup or sugar will be added if you don't specify the ingredients. If you drink gin and tonic, make sure the tonic water contains no sugar. If you prefer Crown and Coke, use Diet Coke. In summary, moderate alcohol consumption is okay as long as you make it absolutely sugar-free.

Excess sugar is your enemy. It is the enemy of weight control. It is also the enemy of staying young.

Making the right choices can get tricky. For instance, restaurant and store-bought meatballs are commonly made with bread. If I want meatballs, I make them from scratch so I am certain that they are all-meat. I never eat bread or chips served as a "free" pre-meal appetizer. There's a reason that some restaurants offer high-sugar appetizers at no cost. The customers mindlessly snack on these foods as they select and wait for their entree. They end up ordering more and eating more and the restaurant makes more money.

When you select your meal, keep in mind that you are never counting calories. You are simply staying away from sugar. Grams of sugar per serving should be the only metric used when determining which foods to eat.

You will need to refuse all desserts except berries and whole whipped cream. This is a low-sugar dish that satisfies the sweet tooth. Avoid alcoholic dessert beverages as well. You may have tea or an after-dinner coffee, but use Splenda instead of sugar.

Here are some useful tips for dining at your favorite places.

Steakhouse

Going to a steakhouse always makes me happy. It is relatively easy to order a healthy and satisfying meal. Always ask the server not to bring any bread to the table. Acceptable appetizers include shrimp or other shellfish, salads with sugar-free dressings, and vegetables of any kind. It is okay to use butter on your vegetables because butter itself is a low-sugar food.

None of your meals can be fried, so appetizers such as fried calamari are on the Not Okay List. Steer clear of any bread or potatoes. The blessing here is that you can order any steak that you want.

Okay List	Not Okay List
Any Steak (cooked any way you like)	A1 Steak Sauce
Any Vegetables	Any Sauce with Sugar
Berries and Cream (Limited)	Anything Fried
Chicken	Bread
Coffee	Candied Carrots
Creamed Spinach	Candied Nuts
Diet Soda	Desserts
Fish	Fries
Lobster	Potatoes
Salad (with sugar-free dressing)	Regular Beer
Shellfish	Soda
Steamed Broccoli	
Ultra-Light Beer (Very Limited)	
Wine, after 6 months (Very Limited)	

Italian

Italian may be one of the more difficult cuisines to eat. Be sure to ask your server not to bring any bread to the table. Avoid fried foods and anything with pasta. Do not order anything with a thick crust, such as pizza, calzones, and garlic knots. Shellfish or a salad with sugar-free dressing is a great start to your meal. Be careful if you choose to drink wine.

Okay List	Not Okay List
Berries and Cream (Limited)	All Pasta
Cheese	Anything Fried
Chicken Marsala	Bread
Diet Soda	Chicken Parmesan
Fish	Desserts
Parmesan	Lasagna
Salad (with sugar-free dressing)	Manicotti
Shellfish	Pizza
Ultra-Light Beer (Very Limited)	Regular Beer
Veal Marsala	Soda
Vegetables	Spaghetti and Meatballs
Wine, after 6 months (Very Limited)	Stuffed Shells
	Subs

Mexican

Mexican foods may contain large quantities of carbohydrates. Stay away from tortillas, taco shells, and anything made with corn. Feel free to eat plenty of meat, fish, cheeses, salsa, and other sauces. You can still enjoy a spicy dinner without a mountain of rice. If you're really feeling the fiesta, go salsa-dancing afterward!

Okay List	Not Okay List
Any Meat, Fish, Chicken, Beans with Cheese (no rice)	All Rice-Based Dishes

Any Vegetables (not fried, no rice)	All Sugary Beverages
Diet Soda	Anything Fried
Fajitas (no tortillas)	Anything Made with Corn
Queso	Anything with Tortilla or Shell
Salad (with sugar-free dressing)	Chips
Salsa and Other Tomato-Based Sauces	Desserts
Shellfish	Enchiladas
Ultra-Light Beer (Very Limited)	Margaritas
Wine, after 6 months (Very Limited)	Regular Beer
	Tacos

Barbeque

The great thing about barbeques, whether you are at a restaurant or at a friend's house, is that they are certainly fun! You get to eat like a kid, with your elbows on the table and sauce staining your clothes. They do offer a lot of meats, so you can eat heartily as long as you don't add any barbeque sauce. The meat is marinated prior to cooking, so it should be flavorful anyway.

Green beans and baked beans are fine, as long as they are not dripping in a sugary sauce. Steer clear of corn, biscuits, and heavy beers.

Okay List	Not Okay List
Beans (little or no sugar in sauce)	A1 Steak Sauce
Berries and Cream (Limited)	All Potatoes
Beef	Anything Fried
Chicken	Barbeque Sauce (with sugar added)
Coleslaw (Limited)	Biscuits
Collard Greens	Bread
Diet Soda	Desserts
Pork	Regular Beer
Salad (with sugar-free dressing)	Soda
Ultra-Light Beer (Very Limited)	

Wine, after 6 months (Very Limited)	

Chinese

Many people assume that any Asian-inspired food is healthy. This simply is not the case. In other countries, the food is prepared differently than how an American restaurant makes it. Stay away from fried foods, rice, noodles, and fortune cookies. Order a soup or salad, but no dressing. The ginger dressing at Chinese restaurants typically has a lot of sugar.

Okay List	Not Okay List
Any Soup	Anything Fried
Beef with Vegetables	Anything Made with Sugary Sauces
Chicken with Vegetables	Desserts
Diet Soda	Dumplings
Pork with Vegetables	Fortune Cookies
Salad (with sugar-free dressing)	Noodles
Shrimp with Vegetables	Regular Beer
Ultra-Light Beer (Very Limited)	Rice
Wine, after 6 months (Very Limited)	Soda

Japanese

Contrary to popular belief, sushi is not necessarily healthy for you. All of the sticky rice layered onto American sushi will not help your waistline. Avoid seaweed salad, noodles, and anything fried. Do not order sake. Feel free to load up on hibachi-cooked foods, sashimi, and soy sauce with wasabi. The wasabi is great for clearing a stuffy nose!

Okay List	Not Okay List
Any Soup	Anything Fried
Any Vegetables	Anything Made with Rice

Beef	Anything Made with Sugary Sauces
Chicken	Desserts
Diet Soda	Noodles
Fish	Regular Beer
Hibachi-cooked foods (without rice)	Sake
Pork	Seaweed Salad
Salad (with sugar-free dressing)	Soda
Sashimi	Sushi
Shellfish	
Soy Sauce	
Ultra-Light Beer (Very Limited)	
Wasabi	
Wine, after 6 months (Very Limited)	

Exercise Quiz

TRUE OR FALSE

1. If you can run a marathon, that means you are really healthy.

2. Cycling for 3 hours is a great way to get cardio and should be done as often as possible.

3. Weight lifting is more important for men than it is for women.

4. It is impossible to exercise too much.

5. Lifting weights helps keep bones strong.

6. Endurance sports are the best form of exercise to look and feel young.

7. You can't get injured if you do the same cardio work-out every day.

8. Weight lifting and cardio exercise burn the same amount of calories.

9. When weight lifting, you should try to rest for 30 seconds or less between sets.

10. Stretching is not important.

11. If you lift weights, you will probably bulk up and look "beefy."

12. Weight lifting offers heart health benefits.

13. You can't get injured if you stick to the same weight lifting routines.

14. If you do a ton of cardio, you can eat whatever you want without gaining weight.

15. It doesn't matter how focused you are when you work out.

16. Taking the stairs instead of the elevator is a good idea.

17. If you can bike more than 50 miles at a time, you must have a very healthy heart.

18. The body burns more calories for 24 hours after lifting weights.

19. Intense weight lifting has anti-aging benefits.

20. If you only lift weights, you will probably gain weight.

21. Long-endurance exercise causes physical stress on the body.

22. People who exercise an excessive amount are addicted in a way that is similar to drug addiction.

23. Lengthy cardio exercise, such as running a marathon, can cause very small heart attacks.

24. Rest is not an important part of an exercise regimen.

25. Weight lifting increases your resting metabolism.

CHAPTER 4

The Truth about Endurance

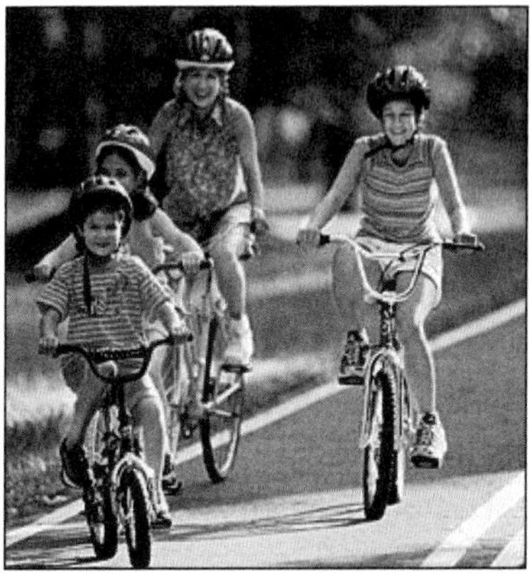

What's the longest distance you've ever biked? How far and how long can you swim at a steady pace? Have you ever run a marathon? Believe it or not, this focus on cardiovascular endurance is nothing more than a product of our society. It is not all that healthy for you.

I repeat: long hours of endurance exercise are not healthy for you.

Physical activity is important. You should easily be able to climb the stairs at work or home. If you are feeling out of breathe after a single flight of stairs, you should visit your doctor.

However, cardiovascular exercise is not meant to be a 40-mile bike ride. Long distance endurance excursions are fun for some people. In fact, some people make a day of it individually or as a group; this can become an addictive behavior as the body produces opiods (narcotics) in response to the stress which this activity causes to your body. Athletes and people who do intense long aerobic exercise often experience overuse syndromes including joint pain, tendonitis, and chronic fatigue. If you partake in such exercise you may eat things loaded in sugar, like Bear-Naked Granola. These food items are labeled as "organic" and "healthy," yet they contain over 8 grams of sugar per serving. Remember, sugar is toxic to your bloodstream. This activity promotes behavior similar to drug addiction.

As one of those really motivated people, I know what it's like to push your limits. You always want to see if you can ride a little farther than you did last time. That's part of the problem. You bike those 40 miles, and the next time you try to ride 60 miles. After that, you're trying to bike 100 miles in one trip, and when you are done your body wants to give out on you.

Being healthy is important. But excessive cardiovascular exercise can lead to wear and tear on the joints, muscles, and other systems.

Heart Health

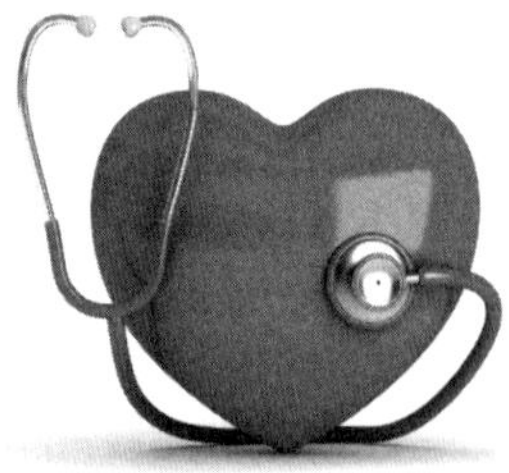

A lengthy cardiovascular workout can damage your heart. Studies have shown that people experience myocardial infarcts during long-distance training, such as running a marathon. Myocardial infarcts are like small heart attacks. They are not a medical emergency, but they are not good for your heart. This excessive focus on cardio, such as biking for 3 hours straight, places strain on the heart muscle. The tissues are damaged, and the physical stress causes miniature heart attacks. Almost everyone has experienced a myocardial infarct, but they do not know it.

When I mention riding your bike for 3 hours, I am not talking about taking a leisurely afternoon ride. That would be a great type of light cardio or fun physical activity! The heart damage that I am talking about comes from running, swimming, biking, and any other endurance-focused activity, for 2 or more intensive training hours. You are stressing your body out, which causes it to age faster. Exercise moderately a little bit each day is far better than a long spurt of high endurance activity.

Hormones and Exercise

Health, in many ways, is the same thing as youth. Growth and reproductive hormones are directly related to youth. Studies have shown that these hormones fluctuate depending on the type of exercise you are doing.

When you do a lot of cardio, you are essentially decreasing your "youth hormone" production. Testosterone levels are especially low in males after cardiovascular training. Estrogen and progesterone levels are very low in women after cardio exercise. This unwanted effect gets worse with age.

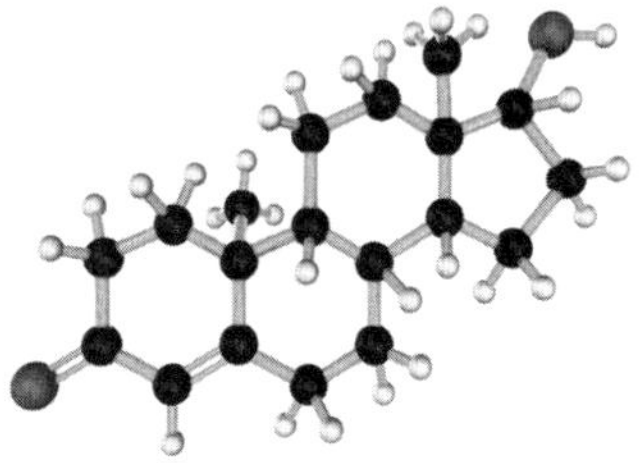

If you focus on weight lifting, you can increase your growth and reproductive hormone levels. You will build lean muscle mass and lose fat. This means your metabolism will increase, and you will burn more calories even while sitting. You will have more energy. You're going to look, and feel, younger. You're going to be healthier.

Your body releases endorphins no matter what type of physical activity you are doing. Weight lifting, running, and walking around a theme park, endorphins are released in response to your physical motion. They are feel-good hormones, and they make you happy. If you exercise too much, your body becomes addicted to this endorphin high. This is how people wind up biking 100 miles, thinking that they're doing something really healthy.

Excessive training also generates cortisol, a stress hormone. This contributes to that exhausted, completely drained feeling you get after a very long run. You can't move your limbs, and you may be in pain. You might even have a headache or minor chest discomfort. The extreme cardio exercise stressed out your body and it is trying to recover.

CHAPTER 5

Training for Sports

Most athletes have a great physique, but they have made a choice to commit their body to a certain type of lifestyle. If you meet someone over 40, who has committed their life to a sport, ask them about the surgeries they have already had and the ones they will need. The list is long, and it's not exactly fun.

I'm not saying you can never do cardiovascular exercise. I am saying that if you want to commit to a sport or some other endurance training, understand what you are accepting for your future medical needs. Be honest with yourself, and admit that you are doing the endurance sport because you want to. The intensive cardio work is not for your health, it is for fun. It is because you love it.

This is quite the paradigm shift for a lot of people. As a physician trained in molecular biology, it is my job to help educate people to be healthier. You may have believed that setting big goals such as running a marathon or biking 50 miles is going to make you healthier. But, surgery as a result of a worn out joint, or torn muscle, could undo years of fitness training.

I propose a moderate fitness plan, with daily or three times daily exercise. Don't stress your body more than you need to.

A Better Way to Workout

Shorter sets of cardio, such as 20 to 30 minutes on the elliptical, are less damaging to your joints and the rest of your body. About two times a week women may want to plan for some light cardio. Men can find it useful as well, but I have repeatedly found that my female patients appreciate the effects of cardiovascular activity more.

If you are weight training the right way, it is actually aerobic exercise as well and is healthy for your heart. When I lift weights, I have scheduled pauses between sets. During those breaks, I do not sit around. I simply switch to a short burst of abdominal work, such as crunches or holding a plank. This keeps the heart-rate up and adds that aerobic quality to your muscle-building routine.

Exercise Regimen

We're going to think big then break it down into smaller sections. We'll even go over a few examples of exercises you can do at home. Please check with your family practitioner about any health concerns prior to beginning new physical activity.

3-Month Outline

Here is a suggested 3-month schedule that you may follow from home or at the gym. It is a general outline that works for both males and females. As the calendar suggests, by the end of 3 months you will be able to adjust your training schedule to fit your personal needs. Always rotate which muscle groups you are using. Do not rest more than 2 days a week. Do not schedule cardiovascular exercise more than 2 times a week.

I have set aside Sundays of each week for strictly rest or leisurely-types of physical activity. It is important to schedule time for fun activities to keep your new habits manageable. This balance is crucial if you want to make permanent improvements. To suit your personal needs, you should consider which day you feel is most important to keep open.

1st Month

SUN	MON	TUES	WEDS	THURS	FRI	SAT
Rest	-Chest -Biceps -Abs	-Light Cardio -Abs	-Back -Shoulders -Triceps -Abs	Rest	-Quads -Ham-strings -Glutes -Abs	-Inner Thighs -Outer Thighs -Abs, Focus on Obliques
Light Cardio or Fun Physical Activity	Rest	-Chest -Biceps -Abs	-Back -Shoulders -Triceps -Abs	-Quads -Hamstrings -Glutes -Abs	Rest	-Inner Thighs -Outer Thighs -Abs, Focus on Obliques
Light Cardio or Fun Physical Activity	-Chest -Biceps -Abs	Rest	-Back -Shoulders -Triceps -Abs	-Quads -Hamstrings -Glutes -Abs	-Inner Thighs -Outer Thighs -Abs, Focus on Obliques	Rest
Light Cardio or Fun Physical Activity	-Chest -Biceps -Abs	-Back -Shoulders -Triceps -Abs	Rest	-Quads -Hamstrings -Glutes -Abs	-Inner Thighs -Outer Thighs -Abs, Focus on Obliques	-Light Cardio -Abs
Rest	-Chest -Biceps -Abs	-Back -Shoulders -Triceps -Abs				

2nd Month

SUN	MON	TUES	WEDS	THURS	FRI	SAT
			-Quads -Hamstrings -Glutes -Abs	Rest	-Inner Thighs -Outer Thighs -Abs, Focus on Obliques	-Chest -Biceps -Abs
Light Cardio or Fun Physical Activity	-Back -Shoulders -Triceps -Abs	Rest	-Quads -Hamstrings -Glutes -Abs	-Light Cardio -Abs	-Inner Thighs -Outer Thighs -Abs, Focus on Obliques	-Chest -Biceps -Abs
Rest	-Back -Shoulders -Triceps -Abs	-Quads -Hamstrings -Glutes -Abs	-Inner Thighs -Outer Thighs -Abs, Focus on Obliques	-Chest -Biceps -Abs	Rest	-Light Cardio -Abs
Rest	-Back -Shoulders -Triceps -Abs	-Quads -Hamstrings -Glutes -Abs	-Inner Thighs -Outer Thighs -Abs, Focus on Obliques	Rest	-Chest -Biceps -Abs	-Back -Shoulders -Triceps -Abs
Light Cardio or Fun Physical Activity	-Quads -Hamstrings -Glutes -Abs	Rest	-Inner Thighs -Outer Thighs -Abs, Focus on Obliques	-Chest -Biceps -Abs	-Back -Shoulders -Triceps -Abs	

3rd Month

SUN	MON	TUES	WEDS	THURS	FRI	SAT
						Rest
Light Cardio or Fun Physical Activity	-Quads -Hamstrings -Glutes -Abs	-Inner Thighs -Outer Thighs -Abs, Focus on Obliques	-Chest -Biceps -Abs	Rest	-Back -Shoulders -Triceps -Abs	-Quads -Hamstrings -Glutes -Abs
Light Cardio or Fun Physical Activity	Rest	-Inner Thighs -Outer Thighs -Abs, Focus on Obliques	-Chest -Biceps -Abs	-Back -Shoulders -Triceps -Abs	Rest	-Quads -Hamstrings -Glutes -Abs
Light Cardio or Fun Physical Activity	-Inner Thighs -Outer Thighs -Abs, Focus on Obliques	Rest	-Chest -Biceps -Abs	-Back -Shoulders -Triceps -Abs	-Quads -Hamstrings -Glutes -Abs	-Inner Thighs -Outer Thighs -Abs, Focus on Obliques
Rest	-Chest -Biceps -Abs	-Back -Shoulders -Triceps -Abs	-Quads -Hamstrings -Glutes -Abs	Rest	-Inner Thighs -Outer Thighs -Abs, Focus on Obliques	-Light Cardio -Abs

Muscle-Building Examples

The 3-month outline is a useful tool for viewing your new lifestyle in a permanent, manageable manner. However, it does not offer any details on how you should condition specific muscle groups. This section offers a full week of exercises that you can do from home. Feel free to use weight lifting machines at a gym instead if you can afford a membership. Each machine should specify which muscles are being used.

Chest and Upper Back

Wide Push-Ups: No weights required. While lying in a face-down position, place hands on floor, several inches outside each shoulder. You may want to use something stable and soft under your hands to cushion the floor for your wrists. While keeping body flat, press yourself up into a plank position. Keep eyes focused on floor about 1 foot in front of you and make sure body is in a straight line. Slowly bend arms to lower your body closer to the ground. Try to touch your nose to the floor, but do not let arms bend past an angle of 90 degrees. While keeping body in a straight line, press back up. Focus on the inward pull of your elbows.

1. This is 1 wide push-up. Do 10 repetitions for 1 set. Switch to 30 seconds of abs. Do another set of wide push-ups.
2. For beginners, try doing these with your knees on the floor instead of your feet. Keep body in a straight line.
3. For advanced training, increase number of repetitions and number of sets.

Chest and Shoulders

Arm Press: Weights or 2 heavy objects required. Stand with feet no more than shoulder-width apart. Never lock knees. Hold 1 weight in

each hand. Bend arms forward to 90-degree angles, so weights are perpendicular to floor in front of body. Keep abs braced and shoulders rolled back, down and away from neck. Keep back straight. Focus on object straight ahead at eye-level. Keeping arms bent at 90-degree angles, raise elbows from sides of body. The line from your shoulder to your elbow should be parallel with the floor. Keep wrists straight. Raise hands up towards ceiling by pivoting shoulders and maintaining 90-degree angles. Press arms towards one another in front of your body, maintaining 90-degree angles. Do not let arms touch. Pull arms back out to sides. Lower hands back to elbow-height. Lower elbows to sides, returning to starting position.

1. This is 1 arm press. Do 12 repetitions for 1 set. Switch to 30 seconds of abs. Do another set of arm presses.
2. For beginners, try doing these with very light weights.
3. For advanced training, increase weight, number of repetitions, and number of sets.

Biceps and Upper Back

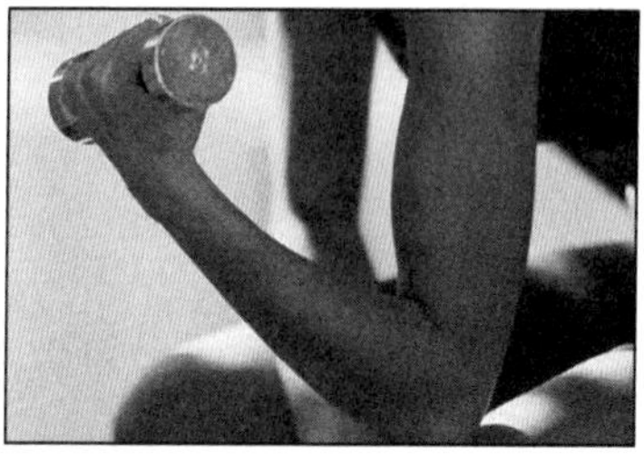

Bicep Curls: Weights or 2 heavy objects required. Stand with feet no more than shoulder-width apart. Never lock knees. Hold 1 weight in each hand, palms facing forward. Keep abs braced and shoulders rolled back, down and away from neck. Keep back straight. Focus on object straight ahead at eye-level. Keeping upper body and shoulders still, bend arms to raise hands in front of body. Keep wrists straight. Continue raising hands until weights almost touch shoulders. Slowly lower hands back to sides, keeping upper body and shoulders still.

1. This is 1 bicep curl. Do 12 repetitions for 1 set. Switch to 30 seconds of abs. Do another set of bicep curls.

2. For beginners, try doing these with very light weights or just 1 arm at a time.
3. For advanced training, increase weight, number of repetitions, and number of sets.

Triceps and Upper Back

Tricep Push-Ups: No weights required. While lying in a face-down position, place hands on floor directly under shoulders. Arms should bend straight back, keeping elbows alongside body. You may want to use something stable and soft under your hands to cushion the floor for your wrists. While keeping body flat, press yourself up into a plank position. Keep eyes focused on floor about 1 foot in front of you and make sure body is in a straight line. Slowly bend arms to lower your body closer to the ground. Keep arms close against your body. Elbows should be pointing directly backward, with insides of arms touching your body. Try to touch your nose to the floor. Press back up. Focus on the forward and backward pull of your elbows.

1. This is 1 tricep push-up. Do 10 repetitions for 1 set. Switch to 30 seconds of abs. Do another set of tricep push-ups.
2. For beginners, try doing these with your knees on the floor instead of your feet. Keep body in a straight line.
3. For advanced training, increase number of repetitions and number of sets.

Triceps

Tricep Raises: Weights or 2 heavy objects required. Stand with feet no more than shoulder-width apart. Never lock knees. Hold 1 weight in each hand with weights parallel to floor. Keep abs braced and shoulders rolled back, down and away from neck. Keep back straight. Focus on object straight ahead, at eye-level. Keeping upper body and shoul-

ders still, bend arms to raise elbows behind your body. Arms should be bent at 90-degree angles with weights held parallel to floor. Straighten arms directly behind body, in an attempt to make entire arms parallel to floor. Keep writs straight. Pause. Slowly lower hands down, returning to starting position, with arms bent at 90-degree angles behind body.

1. This is 1 tricep raise. Do 10 repetitions for 1 set. Switch to 30 seconds of abs. Do another set of arm presses.
2. For beginners, try doing these with very light weights or just 1 arm at a time.
3. For advanced training, increase weight, number of repetitions, and number of sets.

Quads, Hamstrings, and Glutes

Lunges: No weights required. Stand with feet no more than hip-width apart. Never lock knees. Keep abs braced and shoulders rolled back, down and away from neck. Keep back straight. Focus on object straight ahead at eye-level. Keeping upper body still, step one foot forward. Slowly bend knees and lower body close to ground. Front and back knees should bend to 90-degree angles. Do not touch back knee to floor. Slowly raise body back up and step feet back together, without locking knees.

1. This is 1 lunge. Do 15 repetitions with each leg for 1 set. Switch to 30 seconds of abs. Do another set of lunges.
2. For beginners, start out with 10 repetitions on each leg per set. Increase number of repetitions each week.
3. For advanced training, increase number of repetitions and num-

ber of sets. Try stepping foot backward or at 45-degree angles, instead of directly in front of your body. Option of holding 1 weight in each hand during sets. Keep weight balanced.
4. For very advanced training, step foot directly forward and jump to switch legs when knees are both bent at 90-degree angles. Allow body to fully lower so that knees both reach 90-degree angles. Jump again to switch back to first side, allowing knees to reach 90-degree angles. This is one full repetition that uses both legs. Do 15 repetitions. Switch to 30 seconds of abs. Do another set of jumping lunges.

Quads, Hamstrings, Glutes, and Outer Thighs

Side Lunges: No weights required. Stand with feet no more than hip-width apart. Never lock knees. Keep abs braced and shoulders rolled back, down and away from neck. Keep back straight. Focus on object straight ahead, at eye-level. Keeping upper body still, step right foot directly out to right side. Bend right knee to a 90-degree angle, lowering body down and to the right. Allow left leg to straighten, but do not lock your knee. Keep upper body elevated. Slowly straighten right leg to push body back up. Bring right leg back in, next to left. Feet should again be hip-width apart.

1. This is 1 side lunge. Do 15 repetitions with each leg for 1 set. Switch to 30 seconds of abs. Do another set of side lunges.
2. For beginners, start out with 10 repetitions on each leg per set. Increase number of repetitions each week.
3. For advanced training, increase number of repetitions and number of sets. Option of holding 1 weight in each hand during sets. Keep weight balanced.
4. For very advanced training, do not place leg back on floor between repetitions. After lunging to the side and pushing off floor with

right leg, bring right leg in next to left leg. Hold right leg in a bent position, so right foot is in line with left knee. Lunge back out to the side from this position. Do 15 repetitions with each leg for 1 set. Switch to 30 seconds of abs. Do another set of balancing side lunges.

Hamstrings, Glutes, and Lower Back

Hip Raises: No weights required. While lying on your back on the floor, bend legs and place arms by sides. Palms should face down. Keep feet hip-width apart. Place feet as close to your butt as possible. Everyone has a distance that is most comfortable for their knees, so take the time to find the correct placement of your feet. The distance may be anywhere from a couple inches to 1 foot away from your butt. Keep eyes focused on area of ceiling directly above your head. Keep abs braced and shoulders rolled back, down and away from neck. Keeping upper body still, slowly raise hips off of floor. Knees should be close to 90-degree angles. You should be pressing down on the floor with your heels. If you touch the muscles, you should feel tension in your lower back, glutes, and hamstrings. Do not press down on floor with hands. Pause with hips raised. Slowly bend knees to lower body back to starting position on the ground.

1. This is 1 hip raise. Do 12 repetitions for 1 set. Switch to 30 seconds of abs. Do another set of hip raises.
2. For beginners, start out with 10 repetitions per set and increase number of repetitions each week.
3. For advanced training, increase number of repetitions and number of sets. Option of holding 1 weight on pelvis during sets. Option of placing feet with toes angled slightly inward, straight ahead, or slightly outward.
4. For very advanced training, try doing these with one leg at a time. Raise leg that is not being used and hold parallel to floor. Do 12 repetitions on each leg for 1 set. Switch to 30 seconds of abs. Do another set of single-leg hip raises.

Inner Thighs

Inner Thigh Raises: No weights required. While lying on your side on the floor, straighten legs away from body. Bend arm that is closest to floor to prop your head up. Place other arm at a 90-degree angle in front of upper body for support. Bend top leg that is farthest from floor and place in front of lower body. The foot of this leg should be in line with the knee of the bottom straightened leg. It may be useful to maintain a focus on your legs so you can watch your form during this exercise. Slowly lift bottom leg with inner thigh muscles. Keep bottom leg straight, but do not lock your knee. Toes do not need to be pointed. There is no need to lift leg very high. Do not press on floor with upper body or hand. Brace abdominals to keep upper body still. Pause and hover leg above floor, pressing down through heel of top leg to maintain stability. Slowly lower straightened leg to floor, without actually resting straightened leg on floor.

1. This is 1 inner thigh raise. Do 15 repetitions with each leg for 1 set. Switch to 30 seconds of abs. Do another set of inner thigh raises.
2. For beginners, start out with 10 repetitions per set and increase number of repetitions each week.
3. For advanced training, increase number of repetitions and number of sets. Option of using light ankle weight during sets. Option of performing extra sets with pointed or flexed feet.

Upper and Lower Back

Supermans: No weights required. While lying facedown on the floor, extend arms and legs away from body. Arms should be shoulder-width apart with palms facing up. Feet should be hip-width apart with toes straightened flat on floor. Never lock knees. Keep neck elongated, with shoulders down away from ears and face straight down on floor. Keep abs braced. You may want to use something stable and soft under the trunk of your body to cushion chest and pelvis areas. Keeping

focus on floor, use center back muscles to raise both arms and both legs off of floor. There is no need to lift them very high. Pause and hover above the floor for a moment. Slowly lower both arms and both legs back to floor, returning to start position.

1. This is 1 superman. Do 15 repetitions for 1 set. Switch to 30 seconds of abs. Do another set of supermans.
2. For beginners, start out with 10 repetitions per set and increase number of repetitions each week. Option of only raising either arms or legs at a time. Raising only arms will exercise upper back muscles. Raising only legs will exercise lower back muscles. Do at least 10 repetitions for upper back and lower back for 1 set. Switch to 30 seconds of abs. Do another set of half-supermans.
3. For advanced training, increase number of repetitions and number of sets. Option of using light wrist or ankle weights during sets.

Upper Abdominals

Crunches: No weights required. While lying on your back on the floor, bend legs to comfortable position feet behind butt. Keep feet hip-width apart and flat on floor. Keep lower back and spine pressed against floor. It may help to think of tilting your pelvis upward. You may want

to use something stable and soft under the trunk of your body to cushion spine and hip bones. Think of pulling your belly-button in to the floor to brace abs. Place hands crossed on chest, or lightly positioned behind neck for support. Keep shoulders down, away from ears. Inhale. Use abdominal muscles to slowly lift your upper body off of the floor while exhaling. Think of shortening the horizontal distance between your chest and hips. Do not pull on head or neck with hands. Pause at top of crunch to finish exhale. Slowly lower upper body back to floor to reach starting position.

1. This is 1 crunch. Do 30 to 60 seconds of crunches between sets of other muscle-building exercises.
2. For beginners, start out with 30 seconds or less per set. Increase amount of time each week.
3. For advanced training, increase amount of time to over 60 seconds. Option of holding a weight on chest during sets. Keep weight still and balanced.
4. For very advanced training, hold legs together at knees and ankles. Lift legs at a 90-degree angle, so that knees are directly above hips. Shins should be parallel to floor. Hold lower body still while crunching chest towards hips for 30 to 60 seconds between sets of other muscle-building exercises.

Lower Abdominals

Leg Lifts: No weights required. While lying on your back on the floor, bend legs to a 90-degree angle. Hold knees and ankles together. Lift feet up off of floor, legs bent at a 90-degree angle. Knees should be directly above hips, and shins should be parallel to floor. Keep lower back and spine pressed against floor. It may help to think of tilting your pelvis upward. You may want to use something stable and soft under the trunk of your body to cushion spine and hipbones. Think of pulling your belly-button in to the floor to brace abs. Place hands flat on floor, palms facing up. Keep shoulders down, away from ears. Inhale as you use abdominal muscles to slowly lower your feet to the floor. Do not touch feet to floor. Do not press against floor with your hands. Keep spine pressed to floor and legs bent at a 90-degree angle. Exhale, using lower abdominal muscles to raise leg back to position with knees directly above hips. Think of tilting your pelvis upward. It should feel as if your legs are connected to a hinge in the center of your stomach. Keep spine pressed to floor and legs bent at a 90-degree angle. Pause to finish

exhale, contracting abdominal muscles as tight as possible.

1. This is 1 leg lift. Do 30 to 60 seconds of leg lifts between sets of other muscle-building exercises.
2. For beginners, start out with 30 seconds or less per set. Increase amount of time each week.
3. For advanced training, increase amount of time to over 60 seconds. Option of straightening legs to anywhere between a 90-degree angle and a 180-degree straight line. Keep spine pressed to floor.

All Core Muscles

Planks: No weights required. While lying in a facedown position, place hands on floor directly under shoulders. Arms should bend straight back, keeping elbows alongside body. You may want to use something stable and soft under your hands to cushion the floor for your wrists. While keeping body flat, straighten your arms and press yourself up. Keep eyes focused on floor about 1 foot in front of you and make sure body is in a straight line. You may want to use something stable and soft under your hands to cushion the floor for your wrists. Hold your position using your abdominal muscles to keep your back flat. Do not allow hips to raise or lower out of straight line with body. Think of pulling your belly-button in to brace abs. Think of shrinking your middle section by tightening and sucking in stomach muscles. Keep shoulders down, away from ears. Inhale and exhale at a steady pace.

1. This is a regular plank. Hold for 30 to 60 seconds between sets of other muscle-building exercises.
2. For beginners, start out with 30 seconds or less per set. Increase amount of time each week. Option of holding plank on elbows. Elbows should be directly under shoulders, with forearms extending straight forward. Hold for 30 to 60 seconds between sets of other

muscle-building exercises.
3. For advanced training, increase amount of time to well over 60 seconds.

Oblique Abdominals

Side Planks: No weights required. While lying on your side on the floor, straighten legs away from body. Using arm closest to floor, press body up and hold with one arm. You may want to use something stable and soft under your hand to cushion the floor for your wrist. Feet should be stacked one on top of the other, toes pointing in front of you with bottoms of feet perpendicular to floor. Keep legs and feet together. Keep body in straight line. Lift upper arm straight above shoulder, pointed towards ceiling. Think of raising bottom hip toward ceiling, and hold as high as possible without breaking form. Think of pulling your belly-button in to keep abs braced. Think of shrinking your middle section by sucking in stomach muscles. Keep shoulders down, away from ears. Inhale and exhale at a steady pace.

1. This is a side plank. Hold for 30 to 60 seconds between sets of other muscle-building exercises.
2. For beginners, start out with 30 seconds or less per set. Increase amount of time each week. Option of holding plank on elbow. Elbow should be directly under shoulder, with forearms extending straight forward. Hold for 30 to 60 seconds between sets of other muscle-building exercises.
3. For advanced training, increase amount of time to well over 60 seconds. Option of lifting top leg to be parallel with floor. Keep stomach sucked in for stability. Hold for 30 to 60 seconds between sets of other muscle-building exercises.

CHAPTER 6

Acceptable Cardio

Cardiovascular exercise is defined as deliberate movement and activity that activates your cardiovascular systems. These are some of the most popular forms of cardiovascular exercise. If there is a specific physical activity that you love doing, such as gardening, feel free to do that instead! Any fun day spent moving around can be considered light physical activity.

Running: No equipment required, but a good pair of running shoes can help. Jog at a steady pace. Do not run for more than 20 to 30 minutes at a time. Be sure to stay hydrated. If running outside, be careful around moving vehicles. Pick a time of day with mild temperature. Not the best cardio option for those with knee, back, or joint problems.

Biking: Pick out a good bike or attend a cycling class at a gym. Cycle at a steady pace. Do not cycle for more than 20 to 30 minutes at a time. Keep chest elevated and abdominals braced. Be sure to stay hydrated. If biking outside, be careful around moving vehicles. Pick a time of day with mild temperature. Not the best cardio option for those with knee, back, or joint problems.

Walking: No equipment required, but a good pair of walking shoes can help. Try to walk as quickly as possible. Keep a steady pace. Do not walk for more than 30 to 40 minutes at a time. Be sure to stay hydrated. If walking outside, be careful around moving vehicles. Pick a time of day with mild temperature. For those with knee, back, or joint pain, this may not be the best option, but it is better than running or biking.

Swimming: No equipment required, but goggles or a swimmer's cap may be helpful. Swim at a steady pace. Do not swim for more than 30 to 40 minutes at a time. Be sure to stay hydrated. If swimming outside, take care to wear sunscreen with at least an SPF of 15. Good cardio option for those with back problems or joint pain.

Elliptical: This is a cardiovascular machine found in many gyms. You may purchase one for home as well. Try different levels of resistance and inclines. Keep a steady pace. Do not use an elliptical for more than 30 to 40 minutes at a time. Be sure to stay hydrated. Good cardio option for those with back problems or joint pain.

Other examples of cardiovascular activity include chasing your kids around the house, or running stairs at work.

Cardiovascular activity is important and there are several benefits. If you've been an addictive runner however and you have experienced the runner's high, you may have an incorrect view of cardiovascular exercise because you might feel that if you stop running you'll be completely out of shape. I'm not just referring to running but any activity that you have participated in that might have the ability to stress your cardiovascular system. Running, walking, biking, hiking, and all of those activities are excellent for you. What I'm proposing however, is a shift to a moderate level of cardiovascular activity that is actually sustainable throughout your lifetime.

Instead of striving to run long distances or setting a goal to run a marathon so that you can lose 20 pounds incorporate cardiovascular activity into your week, and make it something that you love to do.

If you don't like running don't run. Chase your kids around or find a way to hike with your spouse or significant other. If you've got some injury such as arthritis or a muscle tear, then find ways to swim. Go to your local pool, find a hotel pool, or join the YMCA if you don't have a pool yourself. If you don't like to swim, find something else that you do like to do. Connect with a friend and walk around your neighborhood every morning or evening. Meet at the park and walk a mile together. Join a fitness group and socialize. If you don't like groups and you don't like to socialize, then run the stairs in your house or at your office. Walk a mile on the treadmill or walk around the mall, but the point is get yourself a healthy habit of cardiovascular activity.

Hopefully by now you're seeing that it's your daily habits that make a difference and that it does not have to be extreme. In fact, extreme is not good. The only thing I want to be extreme about is eliminating sugar from your diet once and for all. Stop counting calories and stop consuming excessive amounts of sugary foods. Start focusing on eating healthy green and colorful vegetables and reducing pastas and breads and other types of sugars from your food intake. This will greatly impact your ability to stay young and be vibrant.

A key point about exercise is that aerobic exercise is simply another addiction, which is endorsed by our culture. In some people it's like a positive reinforcement. The more you do, the more you want to do. But just like any other addiction, there are downsides. Your body produces substances that act on the opiate receptors, the same receptors in your brain that ignites the opiate high.

Runners often experience a high that produces endorphins resulting in what's commonly termed the runner's high.

Endorphins flood the space between nerve cells and can inhibit neurons from firing, which creates an analgesic effect. Endorphins also excite neurons and cause a euphoric outcome.

This cycle is why running can become as addictive as drugs. But how good is it for your body?

When you think about how much time it takes to do intense cardio activity it seems counterproductive. Take a look at a seventy-year-old runner, for instance. They're skin and bones, without much muscle. If they'd just spend three hours a week building muscle, they'd be much better off.

Eating well and gaining muscle is much more beneficial than intense cardiovascular exercise. The paradigm shift is away from aerobics and into whatever exercise is healthy for your longevity. If someone spends hours on the treadmill doing aerobics, yet they don't modify their eating habits they're not going to look different.

What I'm proposing is a low carbohydrate solution for health, combined with weight training. What works is a high protein diet with weight training. It's like a lock and key. If I had one solution for a patient who needed to lose twenty pounds, I'd tell them to stay away from sugar.

Food Quiz

TRUE OR FALSE

1. Watermelon is a great food for losing weight.

2. All the extra fat in beans or nuts will make you fat.

3. A calorie from sweet foods, like candy, is just as filling as a calorie from a decadent meal, such as steak and mushrooms in a cream sauce.

4. A ripe banana and an under-ripe banana cause the same amount of insulin production.

5. To lose weight, you need to cut out all sugar from your eating habits, including fruits such as berries or kiwi.

6. Kiwi is a great source of vitamin C for someone trying to reduce their sugar intake.

7. Shrimp is a high-cholesterol food that is bad for you.

8. Dairy products containing no additional sugar are good for you.

9. For the most part, you can eat however many vegetables you want. They are a great way to get vitamins and minerals without an insulin spike.

10. Bread and oatmeal should be avoided at all costs. These foods have too many carbohydrates.

11. Insulin is a bad hormone that is of no use to the body.

12. If you want to focus your lifestyle on low-sugar habits, you can never drink alcohol.

13. A high level of sugar in the bloodstream is toxic to the body.

14. Insulin is secreted at the same pace all day.

15. When insulin production increases during digestion, it is called an insulin spike.

16. What type of bread causes the lowest insulin spike?

a. Wheat bread
b. Sourdough bread
c. White bread
d. Course barley, whole grain, or multi-grain bread
e. None of the above

17. What type of drink is best for you?

a. Orange juice
b. Grapefruit juice
c. V8 100% vegetable juice
d. Tap water
e. None of the above

18. Which food is the most filling for someone with low-sugar eating habits?

a. Grapefruit
b. Bean sprouts
c. Peanuts
d. Low-fat yogurt
e. None of the above

19. Which type of sweetener is the healthiest?

a. Honey
b. Brown sugar
c. Raw sugar
d. Unbleached cane sugar
e. None of the above

20. What organ secretes insulin in response to high-sugar foods?

a. Stomach
b. Appendix
c. Pancreas
d. Gallbladder
e. None of the above

21. Which fruit causes the highest insulin spike?

a. Orange
b. Banana
c. Apple
d. Strawberries
e. None of the above

22. When reading nutrition labels at the grocery store, what is a good amount of sugar per serving to look for?

a. 5 grams of sugar or less
b. Anything under 8 grams of sugar
c. The amount of sugar per serving doesn't matter
d. 2 grams of sugar or less
e. None of the above

23. When you need help waking up in the morning, you should reach for:

a. Coffee
b. Energy drink
c. Energy bar
d. Soda
e. None of the above

24. What is the healthiest source of calcium?

a. Whole milk, including unsweetened dairy, soy, and almond
b. Yogurt
c. Ice cream
d. Macaroni and cheese
e. None of the above

25. What does insulin regulate within the body?

a. Reproductive processes
b. Bone density
c. Carbohydrate and fat metabolism
d. Temperature
e. None of the above

CHAPTER 7

Stocking the Kitchen

How well do you eat? When a patient arrives in my office sick, in need of healing, the conversation always begins with nutrition.

Let's look at some potential smart-food scenarios based on how I teach friends and patients to eat. The idea behind healthy grocery shopping is to buy enough foods to vary each meal, but to use discipline when selecting these foods. A good understanding of how your body reacts to sugar will help this discipline become a habit.

Be sure to avoid foods with a lot of sugar when you are grocery shopping. Plain sugar is obviously not something you need to keep around. As you read nutrition labels, you'll probably be surprised with the amount of sugar per serving. One serving of bread may have anywhere between 0 to 8 grams of the sweet stuff!

An easy rule of thumb is to avoid items with more than 2 grams of sugar per serving. This can be difficult. You may wind up purchasing a couple items with 3 or 4 grams of sugar per serving. As long as you stick close to the 2 grams, don't sweat it, but don't go overboard, either.

Be honest with yourself. This is supposed to be the beginning of a new, permanent lifestyle. It is a better understanding of how your metabolism works and how your body digests food. It is not meant to be some crash-diet than you can't stand to keep up with.

The most practical start to your low-sugar lifestyle is to follow the Okay and Not Okay Lists found within this book. There is no way around the fact that you have to be strict with your food choices. Prevent the desire to "treat yourself" with the Not Okay List. The resulting insulin rush makes you fat. Low energy and a corresponding increase in appetite makes you want to eat more, even after you've already splurged.

Why so Strict?

Every time you eat something on the Not Okay List, you're making the new habits harder for yourself. When you have a set of foods that you eat regularly, your body is trained to want those foods. If you typically eat steak after lifting weights, your body adapts to the routine. You crave steak every time you finish a work-out. If you eat a giant, bread-stacked sub after exercising, you are more likely to crave that same sub the next time you exercise. It is a combination of chemical triggers released within the body and external factors that remind your brain, "Oh, hey, last time we ate this and it was great! Let's do it again!"

On the bright side, it works this way for all food. Once you have cut back on your sugar intake, you will slowly start to realize that sweet foods do not taste as good as you once thought. Food enthusiasts should be excited about this! Low-sugar lifestyles allow your taste buds to develop more completely. Your taste buds are able to perceive a wider variety of flavor, so you can literally taste the quality of the food you are putting in your mouth.

If you eat mostly healthy foods, you are going to crave those healthy foods. Anything else simply won't taste as good. I've found that you can prepare in advance to succeed.

If someone brings sugary foods to your house, have a plan to get rid of them; don't keep them around. If you're an alcoholic, you wouldn't keep alcohol around, so if you have issues with sugar, don't keep sugar around. Now this might seem radical to all those people who are saying right now, *Come on that's really extreme! I want to have a brownie once in a while.* You can have whatever you want once in a while as long as it's not your lifestyle.

When I talk about being consistent and strict, it's really only about having discipline. This shift in nutrition from a moderately too high sugar intake food consumption to a low to sugar intake consumption can radically transform your life for the better. It is the same way with the shift from a high cardiovascular exercise outlook to a moderate daily cardiovascular exercise mentality. If you're still not convinced about either one step back and think about it. Think about what elderly people look like. Have you ever seen an 80-year-old who's gaunt and thin? Most elderly people have reduced muscle and many seem frail. Think about it: Is high-activity cardiovascular exercise on a repetitive basis going to make you thin and frail or is it going to make you muscular? I am a proponent of weight-bearing exercise and also activity that is healthy for you. Stay active because movement is good. Stay healthy and eat right and reduce your sugar. Both of these things are modifications that you can make today.

But Our Ancestors Ate Foods with Plenty of Sugar!

It is important to understand that if we could be as active as our ancestors were, it would not be necessary to avoid high-sugar foods so completely. We are pretty inactive in modern society. Exercising an hour every day is great, but it is nothing compared to the physical labor of our ancestors. Our society has a sedentary lifestyle because most of us sit at desks all day for work. As a result, we must stay away from foods on the Not Okay List.

Artificial Sweeteners in Food

I do not like sugar alcohols found in food, such as Sorbitol. These are commonly used in low-carbohydrate foods as an artificial. High-protein bars, energy bars, and ice creams frequently contain sugar alcohols like Sorbitol. They can upset your stomach, causing gas and sometimes diarrhea. If you want to feel your best, you should stay away from these as well.

Sugar Substitutes

In contrast, I do like options such as Splenda, Stevia, or Sweet 'n Low. Any sugar substitutes that are derived from sugar are great alternatives. To date, no sugar substitutes have been proven to cause cancer or increase appetite. The well-promoted study, that suggested sugar substitutes may cause cancer, was conducted on lab rats ingesting 5,000 times the recommended amount. Projecting this scale onto humans is unrealistic at best and deceptive at worst.

Organic Foods and Dietary Supplements

I do not believe that organic foods are proven to be healthier than conventionally produced foods, so that choice is up to you. I do not believe in vitamin supplements either. Provided that you eat plenty of foods from the Okay List and you diversify your diet, you should get all of the vitamins and minerals that you need.

Now, I realize that this is radically controversial compared to what many people say. There are some people who believe in alternative medicine who build their entire for-profit practices around supplementation therapy They sell their patients thousands of dollars a month in vitamins and they even use certain machines to test your nutrient levels in the body. You put your hand up against the machine and it tests how high or low the level of nutrients are in your body, and when the levels are low you are prescribed high amounts of supplementation.

Get your blood tested regularly as needed by a well-trained physician and go from there. Once you know what your vitamin level and blood work looks like, you can then get on the appropriate plan for your body.

CHAPTER 8

The Bottom Line

It is up to you to eat healthy. The best way to ensure success is by not allowing high-sugar foods into your house. This prevents the temptation through an out-of-sight, out-of-mind tactic. It is also a good idea, when you are shopping, to avoid the areas of the store where the sweet stuff is kept. There's a giant sign above each aisle. You might as well do yourself and your wallet a favor. Stay away from the aisle that says "cookies, crackers, and other pointless snacks you don't need."

Preparation really is key. You can plan to fail or fail to plan as the saying goes, and I'm here to help you plan for a lifetime of success.

Stock your house with healthy snacks and determine what they are right now. Make a list of healthy snacks. Here's an example: celery, broccoli, carrots, or perhaps fruit. Don't think about higher low-calorie items; think about high or low sugar.

Plan ahead.

Fill your mind with positive empowering material. Buy books, audio, or videos all centered on living a healthy lifestyle. Watch documentaries and buy books that help you think like a healthy person. You will have to continually feed your mind with positive material to help you live a healthier day because each and every day you will be inundated by opposing messages. You will be faced with candy bar commercials, chocolate cake, and a dessert tray at the restaurant after a business dinner. If you say to yourself, *Well it's just this one time*, you'll have a mindset of making small concessions that lead up to big-city subtractions. If on the other hand you decide that you're going to remain committed and firm, then each and every time, you'll be able to say no.

You'll say no to sugar because it will be an automatic mindset that has created an automatic habit and response of saying no.

Remember that the unhealthiest of foods may not look the way you think sugar looks. The most unhealthy food choices might look like an innocent piece of bread or gluten-free pasta. Just make it a routine to say no to anything that makes you feel bloated and anything on the unhealthy food lists within this book. Once you have detoxed your body from sugar and filled your mind and daily routine with positive things, it'll be so easy to keep it up.

Centenarians and have several traits that are believed to cause them to lead healthy lives. Among those traits are interacting with others having a purpose in life and being aware of what they eat and how often they move their bodies.

Do you want longevity? The definition of longevity is when you can think, act, and be who you want to be well into your golden years. Instead of living a sick tired existence where you have no mobility, you can live a happy healthy life and spend time with friends and family doing what they do. You can enjoy traveling to find destinations and going out to wonderful dinners. You can walk by take trips to the beach, create new adventures, write a book, garden, and do whatever else it is that's on your list. You can create whatever kind of life you like to design as long as you plan well.

I wrote this book to inspire you to think about a no-sugar nutrition plan as part of your lifestyle from today forward.

Congratulations on a healthy happy new start!

Lifestyle Quiz

TRUE OR FALSE

1. As an adult, you should get at least 7 hours of sleep a night.
2. Stress-reducing techniques, such as a massage, deep breathing, or yoga, are not important to your overall health and feeling young.
3. Your exact sleep needs are dependent upon personal factors, such as your age and how much sleep you have already missed out on.
4. Putting yourself first means you are selfish, and you should feel guilty about it.
5. Women may experience irregular sleep patterns during pregnancy and menopause.
6. Reading can benefit your memory.
7. Doing other things while you are eating will distract you and make you eat less.
8. Sleep affects your appetite and which foods you crave.
9. Multitasking is a more efficient way to get things done.
10. A teenager needs less sleep than an adult.
11. High school starts early in the morning because teenagers are biologically inclined to wake up early.
12. Listening to music, writing, and reading are all easy and inexpensive ways to decompress after a long day.
13. Exercise is more important than sleep.
14. You should drink alcohol before bed because it will help you sleep.

15. **Only about 2% of humans can actually multitask.** T

16. **Being successful is more important than having healthy and loving relationships.** F

17. **Television and computer screens emit a light that is similar to sunlight, so they should be avoided shortly before bedtime.** T

18. **In today's society, finding a moment to enjoy peace and quiet each day is a good idea.** T

19. **Learning new skills and trying new experiences will not only keep you feeling young, but it could help prevent dementia.** T

20. **Being happy, healthy, and attractive is about being perfect.** F

21. **You don't need to change your way of thinking to change your habits and lifestyle.** F

22. **Pet owners, particularly those with dogs, may experience less stress as a result of the bonds created with their animal pals.** T

23. **If you have kids, you may as well give up on needing any time for yourself.** F

24. **You should always follow societal norms because they seem to work fine for everybody else.** F

25. **Spending a little time outdoors can help regulate your sleep habits and relieve stress.** T

26. **Which of the following is the healthiest way to de-stress?**
    a. Having an ultra-light beer
    b. Going on a shopping spree
    c. Venting to your friend or spouse
    d. Doing something by yourself, possibly with physical activity
    e. None of the above

D

27. During sleep, your brain:

a. Shuts off entirely
b. Barely functions by regulating breathing and temperature
c. Tries to solve problems that arose throughout your day
d. Does not get to rest
e. None of the above

28. The best way to stay alert throughout the day is:

a. Sipping an energy drink
b. Meeting your personal sleep needs every night
c. Having a cup of coffee in the morning and early afternoon
d. Eating a lot of meals
e. None of the above

29. When you learn new skills or habits, your brain:

a. Stays exactly the same
b. Starts to hurt, causing a headache
c. Creates new connections between brain cells, making the new skill or habit easier with time
d. Goes into overdrive, allowing you to permanently replace bad habits with good habits in less than a week
e. None of the above

30. When you eat, you should:

a. Take time to enjoy your food without distraction
b. Listen to your body; it tells you what fuel it needs and when your tank is full
c. Be aware of the sugar content and aim for 2 grams or less per serving
d. Appreciate the ways healthy food can keep you young
e. All of the above

RESULTS and ANSWER KEYS

Diet Quiz Answer Key

1. E. None of the above
2. C. This diet suggests that your body is adapted to the foods eaten by the early human species.
3. D. Eat very little throughout the day and eat one large meal at night.
4. B. Its good-carbs vs. bad-carbs and good-fats vs. bad-fats take on dieting.
5. D. A low-carb diet increases your resting metabolism because it takes more calories for your body to burn fat.
6. False
7. False
8. True
9. True
10. False
11. False
12. False
13. True
14. False
15. False
16. A. One ultra-light beer
17. B. Carrots
18. A. Creamed spinach
19. B. Lamb with roasted peppers and a heavy cream sauce
20. A. Cherries
21. B. Corn
22. B. Potato

23. A. Low-carb ice cream
24. A. Pizza
25. B. Sushi and small seaweed salad

Exercise Quiz Answer Key

1. False
2. False
3. False
4. False
5. True
6. False
7. False
8. False
9. True
10. False
11. False
12. True
13. False
14. False
15. False
16. True
17. False
18. True
19. True
20. False
21. True
22. True
23. True

24. False
25. True

Food Quiz Answer Key

1. False
2. False
3. False
4. False
5. False
6. True
7. False
8. True
9. True
10. False
11. False
12. False
13. True
14. False
15. True
16. D. Course barley, whole grain, or multi-grain bread
17. D. Tap water
18. C. Peanuts
19. E. None of the above
20. C. Pancreas
21. B. Banana
22. D. 2 grams of sugar or less
23. A. Coffee
24. A. Whole milk, including unsweetened dairy, soy, and almond

25. C. Carbohydrate and fat metabolism

Lifestyle Quiz Answer Key

1. True
2. False
3. True
4. False
5. True
6. True
7. False
8. True
9. False
10. False
11. False
12. True
13. False
14. False
15. True
16. False
17. True
18. True
19. True
20. False
21. False
22. True
23. False
24. False
25. True

26. D. Doing something by yourself, possibly with physical activity
27. C. Tries to solve problems that arose throughout your day
28. B. Meeting your personal sleep needs every night
29. C. Creates new connections between brain cells making the new skill or habit easier with time
30. E. All of the above

Diet Quiz Results

If you got:

0-10 Questions Right: You have been misinformed! It's okay, this might simply mean that you've never tried dieting before. That's not necessarily a bad thing, since many people view healthy diets as temporary. There is a lot for you to learn. Read this book and re-take this test. You should see better results next time!

10-20 Questions Right: This isn't that bad! You have apparently tried some type of diet before. Remember, this is a book about a new lifestyle. You will not be temporarily attempting a new diet. This book will break things down for you, so you have no way of losing. Be honest with yourself, and you'll get a higher score next time you take this test!

20-25 Questions Right: Good job! You have clearly read up on your health information. You might as well forget about this book because you have nothing to learn… Just kidding! There is always room for improvement. This book will help reinforce what you already know and probably teach you a few things your past diets have overlooked. Everything is broken down to basics, so you should get a perfect score by the time you finish this book!

Exercise Quiz Results

If you got:

0-10 Questions Right: Either you're a cardio-slave, or you're just not that into exercise. Too much endurance exercise can actually be harmful to your body. While a little bit of cardio is fine, you want to make sure you focus on weight lifting. You'll learn all about that in this book. When you retake this test, you may be surprised at how much you've learned!

10-20 Questions Right: So you know a little about exercise, but nothing extensive? Well, you're reading the right book! The entire chapter devoted to exercise habits will help you connect the dots in your work-out routine. You probably aren't doing enough weight training right now. A good workout plan isn't easy, but this book will help you discover the methods that work best for you. Try everything at least once, and see how you do the next time you take this test!

20-25 Questions Right: Wow, you must spend a lot of time in the gym! Or perhaps you just spend a lot of time reading about the gym? Either way, this book will help you narrow down your exercise routine, so you can get the best results in minimal time. Nobody wants to spend all of their free time working out. Even if you want to look 20 years younger, there's no need for that degree of exercise. This book will keep you focused on the basics, so you'll feel younger and healthier than you have in a long time. After all that hard work, acing this test will be no sweat!

Lifestyle Quiz Results

If you got:

0-10 Questions Right: It's probably safe to assume you don't get enough sleep. As you will learn in this book, sleep is very important for your body. You also probably missed some key points covered in this book. Not to worry, you still have a little more reading to do and you can always go back and review previous sections. When you retake this test, you may be shocked at what information you missed out on!

10-20 Questions Right: So you might get a decent amount of sleep, but perhaps you're placing too much emphasis on exercise. The lifestyle section of this book focuses on general, day-to-day decisions. It may help you understand the last few points you are missing. You can always look back at previous sections for help. By the time you finish this chapter, your score on this test should be significantly higher!

20-30 Questions Right: Someone's been taking notes! Or maybe you knew everything about health to begin with? Either way, it's clear that you are on the right track for maintaining your youth into later years. To really cement your understanding of these health concepts, finish this section and retake this test. You will probably end up with a perfect score!

About the Author

Graduate School:	University of Southern California
Degree:	Ph.D. (Cellular and Molecular Biology)
Thesis:	The Integration Properties of an Oncogenic DNA Virus
Medical School:	University of Colorado School of Medicine
Degree:	M.D.
Honorary:	Graduated with Honors
Certifications:	American Board of Internal Medicine, September 1988
	ABIM Subspecialty Medical Oncology, November 1991
Societies:	Member, Wisconsin Association of Medical Oncologists
	American Cancer Society Fellowship/Research Award Recipient (1989-1990)
	Board Member, the American Cancer Society, Wisconsin 1991-1993
	Member American Society of Clinical Ontology
	Member Texas Medical Society